# MORE ABOUT GODDESSES

## Volume One: Essays

## Tim Kavi

**TiLu Press, LLC**

*For my wife, Jennifer, goddess extraordinaire*

# CONTENTS

# INTRODUCTION

I've been sharing my poetry on the internet since about 2005, first at an online community called MySpace, and then later migrating my poetry and essay writing over to my official writing page/blog. That website (listed at the end of this book in the About Author section) is where I write and share at least some of my current poetry, essays, publication news, and writing rants and raves from time to time.

From the beginning I was encouraged to get published by my readers and this was realized in 2011 with my first collection, *Emerging Goddess*. It was followed by *Ascending Goddess* (2012) and *Lost Love Poems* (2013). Also in 2013, I had an essay published about Walt Whitman. These were all published as eBooks, but most are also available in print versions as well.

Now over time and in particular the last two and a half years, I have regularly posted columns on my blog that features additional information and facts about goddesses. These columns are simply called *More About Goddesses*. The columns are meant to be tie-ins to my poetry which also mentions goddess motifs and themes. What was unexpected, by both myself and my publisher was how popular these columns would become with internet searchers and my readers.

In fact, not only were some of the columns being read hundreds of times in a short period of time after posting, some of the columns have been read thousands of times. In fact, the second column in this book, as of the present time (July 2013), has been viewed almost 6,000 times by itself. Then we started noticing that users were coming to the blog and seeking these columns out, searching for them specifically in order to read them.

We thought it would be interesting and helpful to publish essay collections from time to time that contains most of the columns that had been on the blog up to that point, and also include new columns that have never been on the blog and never will be. That way, readers could get in one resource, the columns that they have read, could get the columns all together easily (in one place), and read some new columns too that have not ever appeared anywhere else than this book. Also, it might attract new readers to the blog and to my poetry, and I sincerely hope, a message of empowerment for them.

For if you want to be a seeker, why not? Do you want to climb the mountain with me? Great, my poems talk about the search for the Goddess! Do you seek to overcome your circumstances and always transcend? Do you seek to free your minds? So, why not? I hope we have made it easier to get all of these essays together, get new ones, and in doing so, to help you while helping you to also support my work! So here's *More About Goddesses, Volume One*-- hope you enjoy it!

One final thing, I often get asked why I write so much about Goddesses. Well, the short reply version is simply to state that it's my belief that one of the great problems in the postmodern world is unbridled patriarchy. I am convinced that the message of the goddess, both as an archetype, and as a collective ideal and role model for both men and women (yes men too as Jung referred to the anima for men), is sorely needed. While I've been warned by other poets not to speak too much about interpreting my own work, I do want to say something more about the Goddess. Can I at least do that?

Some have argued that the idealization of women invites further difficulties for women in particular (and perhaps for men too who embrace the Goddess message), but I differ with this view, at least archetypically in terms of personal transformation, for I see the Goddess as a symbol for empowerment, personal growth and transformation (see Jean Bolen's writing and my teacher, Christine Downing's writings about that), as well as understanding the Goddess as a sacred subject to subject relation in Her own right. Yes, I do think every woman ought to be treated as if she were a Goddess, while reminding ourselves that both women and men are human, and being ever cautious to understand that when we see the Divine in ourselves and

others it is never to take advantage or to expect
something they are not, but rather to see the spark
that is inside of them as a person, that allowing
them to be fully human, compassionate and em-
powered in their place of freedom in the universe,
that we respect them and give everyone the toler-
ance and freedom to be what they are called to become.--Tim Kavi, Shanghai China; July 2013.

# *AMATERASU: SHINTO GODDESS*

Amaterasu is considered a major deity in the Shinto religion and is frequently depicted in Japanese myths. In some writings she is also referred to as Amateru which translates to "shining in heaven." Her full name, Amaterasu-ōmikami, translates to "the great august kami who shines in heaven."

In myths, Amaterasu is known as the sun goddess. She is the sister of Tshkuyomi, the god of the moon and Susanoo, the goddess of the sea and storms. These siblings are descendants of Izanami with Tsukuyomi being washed out of the right eye, Susanoo being washed out of the nose and Amaterasu being washed out of the left eye. Legend has it that anyone who may sit as an Emperor of Japan must be a direct descendant of this goddess.

In writings, Amaterasu and Tsukuyomi rule over the heavens with her reigning over the sun and him ruling over the night. But one day Tsukuyomi killed

Uke Mochi, the goddess of food because he became disgusted as she pulled food from her nose, mouth and rectum. Amaterasu was disgusted by this murder and labeled her brother as evil, resulting in the split between night and day.

Amaterasu is typically worshipped in the Ise Shrine in Honshu. The Naiku or inner shrine is dedicated to her, holding the Yata no Kagami, the sacred mirror that is said to be one of the Imperial Regalia of Japan. Her followers are typically referred to as "the cult of the sun," though this is occasionally referred to as a worship of the sun that stems from pre-archipelago culture rather than a worship of the goddess herself.

The Shikinen Sengu ceremony is held in this shrine every 20 years as a dedication to the goddess. During this ceremony the main buildings that make up the shrine are destroyed and rebuilt in a new location. Then the goddess will be offered new food and clothing. It is said that this ceremony has been carried out at this location since 690 AD.

# *APHRODITE (VENUS), THE GODDESS OF LOVE AND BEAUTY*

There are many stories surrounding the Goddess Aphrodite. The Olympian goddess was usually seen with the winged Eros, and was always a very beautiful woman. She was attributed with a dove, a scallop shell, an apple and a mirror. There were many sculptures and paintings of her that showed her nude.

Some legends tell of how Aphrodite came from the sea foam, which was created by the dismembered parts of Uranus that had been tossed into the sea by Kronos. Home tells us that Aphrodite is actually born of Zeus and Dione, and later stories tell how she was Kronos' and Euonyme's daughter.

No matter what way she came into the world, everyone was always very struck with her beauty once they saw her, and every man desired her for his wife. She was believed to be the mother of every living being. Something of this can be seen in the contest between Typhon and the gods. Here, Aphrodite changed her form into a fish, which was thought to contain the most generative powers.

Because of her ability to excite passion in all the hearts of men and gods from the Greeks' description of her, she used this power to rule over all of living creation. There were several stories where it says that Aphrodite punished the ones who neglected worship of her or hated the power she had, and other stories where she would protect or favor the ones who paid homage to her and got caught up in her beauty.

# *APHRODITE AND THE STORY OF EROS AND PSYCHE*

Aphrodite is often hailed as the goddess of beauty, love, procreation and pleasure. She is also hailed as the protector of sailors as she was born from the sea foam. Aphrodite is the daughter of Zeus and Dione, making her one of the most vital goddesses in Greek mythology.

Given her nature, Aphrodite is a very personal and intimate goddess, invading the secret places of her followers and remaining close to those that are loyal to her. She can easily bring about a feeling of wonder and magic, particularly encouraging a natural feminine power, but Aphrodite is also capable of deceiving the heart when exalting the sensuality of a couple's union as she sees fit.

The nature of Aphrodite and her ability to manipulate the magical or deceptive side of sensuality is noted in her son Eros's union with Psyche. Eros is the god of passionate sexual love while Psyche was a princess that was so beautiful that many treated her like a goddess. Some would even make sacrifices or perform symbolic gestures in her name, which caused much jealousy amongst other goddesses, particularly Aphrodite.

In her jealousy, Aphrodite sent her son Eros to put a spell on Psyche, making her fall in love with the ugliest man on the Earth. When Eros arrived, he was so stunned by Psyche's beauty that he accidentally pricked himself with one of his magical arrows, falling in love with her instantly. Feeling guilty for his deeds, Eros worked to undo the spell and then left. Enraged that her son could not manage this deed, Aphrodite cast a similar spell to seal Psyche's fate.

Concerned that their daughter would marry a monster, they summoned the Fates. They told her parents to take her to a mountain to leave her for her beastly betrothed. Her parents eventually obliged, and Psyche was left on the mountain in her sorrow. Seeing her tears, Zephyr the West Wind took her away to a lush forest in the valley below. Here she wandered until she found a palace with invisible servants and an invisible lover that would care for her.

Psyche was welcome to enjoy these benefits so long as she only united with her lover in darkness. After much time together, Psyche could no longer manage her curiosity and lit a candle to see her lover, Eros. Hurt by her suspicions, Eros flew away. Psyche's suspicions show the conscience's unwillingness to live with a relationship surrounded in darkness. Given this impossible task, Psyche appealed to Aphrodite asking to be reunited with Eros with no conditions.

Aphrodite conceded, provided Psyche enter the underworld and place a drop of Persephone's beauty in a box. Persephone is known as the beauty of the depths because she was taken down to the Underworld to be the bride of Hades. Determined to be reunited with her lover, Psyche completed this final task, achieving a state where the dark anonymity of her previous love and the divine, personal aspects of love could merge.

Eros and Psyche were given one of few wedding ceremonies given in the presence of all the gods on Olympus. The gods celebrated this new union with a great feast that celebrated the union of the soul, and Eros, the representation of sexual love. At this blessed union, Aphrodite danced in celebration.

# *ARTEMIS, GREEK GODDESS OF THE HUNT*

Artemis is the daughter of Zeus and Leto, and the twin sister of Apollo. Her bow and arrows that she would carry were made by Cyclopes and Hephaestus. She is depicted as goddess of the hunt, wild animals and many cities also worshipped her as the goddess of fertility. Artemis is often depicted with the moon above her head and was frequently depicted as being close with Selene, the goddess of the moon. More often she would be depicted as roaming the mountain forests with her nymphs by her side in search of panthers, stags, hinds and lions. In later myths she would assist these animals by protecting their overall well-being while fighting to ensure their safety.

Artemis is also seen as the goddess of chastity. Legend has it that when she was three years old, Artemis asked Zeus to provide her with eternal virginity. All of her close companions were virgins, and she would punish any man who attempted to harm the purity of herself or her companions. In one legend, Actaeon came upon Artemis and her nymphs bathing naked in a pool, and when she saw him watching Artemis transformed him into a stag and sent her hounds after him. She was also known to use her bow to kill those who were known to rape women, including Orion.

Because Artemis was born before her brother Apollo, her mother gifted her the island of Ortygia as thanks for helping her mother to cross the strait of Delos to give birth to Apollo. This legend made Artemis an idol to women going through childbirth. Some cities depicted her as a goddess and protector to those in the midst of the hunt, a mass of contradictions as she brought sudden death alongside the birth of a new life. Because her twin brother was seen as a healing god, many would pray to Artemis for assistance in the healing of gout, rabies or leprosy in hopes that she would appeal to Apollo on their behalf.

These and other legends of Artemis would be honored with lively festivals. Festivals were held throughout Orthia, Brauron, Brauronia and most notably Sparta. As women became of age and reached puberty they would be initiated into the cult of Artemis, although they would be required to leave this cult once they became married. Artemis was not against the realm of marriage, but she chose to be surrounded by those who were pure, so those who chose to engage in marital acts would be required to return her paraphernalia as they took on this new role.

# *ASHERAH, ANCIENT MOTHER GODDESS*

Asherah is a Semitic mother goddess that has been depicted in a number of writings including the Akkadian. She is commonly thought to be identical to Athirat, the Ugaritic goddess. She is also seen in writings throughout Arabia, Israel, Judah and Egypt. In some writings she is referred to as Elath or Qudshu which roughly translates to "holiness."

Asherah has been depicted in a variety of different roles depending on the area where the writings originated. In some writings, Asherah is commonly seen as the consort or wife of El in Ugaritic writings or Anu in Sumerian writings. Due to her association with one of the oldest deities in these writings, Asherah is given a fairly high rank within the pantheon. In some writings she is depicted as being the consort of Baal. In these writings she is referred to as Baalat. Writings throughout the southern areas of Palestine have depicted her as a concert to Yahweh.

She is commonly referred to as a "goddess par excellence," a high mark of praise. When she is discussed in the Book of Jeremiah she is referred to as the Queen of Heaven. She is considered to be the mother to as many as 70 gods that were worshipped throughout Palestine and Syria. In some writings the word *asherah* does not refer to the goddess, but to the wooden pole that is used throughout the ceremonies that worship the goddess.

In artwork, Asherah is commonly depicted as a limbless trunk of a tree that is planted into the ground. Those that worshipped the goddess continued the theme by referring to themselves as groves. When depicted alongside Baal, Asherah is considered a moon goddess to contrast Baal's role as a sun god. In this role Asherah was considered a very sensual goddess, often worshipped with elaborate rituals that included fortune telling, prostitution and divination. Her role has slowly been removed from much of religious use with the rise of contemporary religions which limited her depiction in later writings.

Some contemporary thinkers refer to her as a forerunner to the concept of Shekinah, if not the embodiment of Shekinah.

# *ATHENA, GREEK GODDESS OF WISDOM AND WAR*

The Greek goddess Athena, often portrayed as full of mercy, strong, and fair, skill and endeavor, is also considered the goddess of heroes and the heroic journey. Also viewed as a representative of Divine Intelligence, and as a goddess of warfare, she was considered the patron goddess of Athens. According to legend, she had quite an unusual birth. Her father, Zeus, ate his first wife, Metis, because he feared when she became pregnant that she had in her womb the son that was prophesied to usurp him of his own throne. This caused him a great headache, worse than any other, and to be rid of it he let another god open up his head. At this moment, it is said that Athena sprang forth from the forehead of Zeus and she was fully clothed in the attire of war.

So, it was not the son he feared that came out

– rather his beautiful, full grown daughter Athena, already dressed in full golden body armor that was "born". Athena became Zeus' favorite child, motherless as she was. She was the only one that he told his secret of where to find his lightning bolts, plus she was trusted to guard his magic shield.

Generally, Athena is seen with a spear in her hand, and her helmet of gold tipped to show her beauty. Although she was dressed for battle, she was much more known for her job as diplomat, judge and mediator. People knew her for her fair and compassionate decisions. Stories also tell of how she helped many other gods, goddesses and heroes out when they were faced with a great problem that seemed impossible.

She was probably the start to the first independent woman. Referred to as a virgin, she was not swayed by Aphrodite, and she stayed independent of all of the responsibilities of marriage and being a mother. You did not hear of romance or marriage in Athena's story.

In Roman mythology, she is known as Minerva, and according to Plato she is also prefigured by the Egyptian goddess Neith.

# *ATHENA: QUEEN OF THE AIR AND BREATH OF INSPIRATION*

Athena is commonly known as the goddess of wisdom, but in her early inspirations she was associated with wind and storms. Like the wind, Athena was portrayed as being cool and clear, which later led to depictions of her being clear, rational and objective. As a goddess who was focused on the strength of mind rather than the strength of body, she eventually lost her association with weather and became a figure associated with inspiration.

In Greek culture, it was believed that the organs which were located higher on the body were more important. This meant that the brain or the mind was the most vital organ in the body, making a goddess like Athena especially important to their culture. Mythology reveals her to be the favorite daughter of Zeus, one of the most powerful characters in the religion. She would often show favor to those who were shown to be shrewd, industrious or moral. These associations made it natural for her to be used as a symbol of inspiration for thoughtful members of Greek society.

Athena was often known to teach the Greeks about aspects of technology which would help improve their society. One of the most well-known examples of this was the creation of a navy which helped the Greeks win many important battles to help preserve their land. This type of work combined her role as a goddess of inspiration and the wind, since both were needed to create and power the vessels.

Athena is often portrayed as an owl, due to her association with wisdom. Owls are known to be very shrewd and cunning animals, making it the ideal fit for a goddess thought to offer battle tactics, philosophy and other bits of inspiration to those she favored. The owl was also a creature known for soaring quickly to hunt and maneuver, which once again ties in the original idea of associating Athena with wind or storms.

This goddess, among many others, is associated with battle due to her tendency to offer tactics to the sides she favored. Because of this, Athena is often depicted as a strong woman, more often than not a warrior watching over her people. Her goal was often to restore peace to troubled lands so that society could continue to grow and prosper, creating beautiful works of art and inventing new forms of technology. She would also act as a muse for artists and craftsmen. It was not uncommon to associate those who did especially well at their craft with the work of Athena.

Above all, Athena would always strive to bring order where there was none. Like the wind, she would gently cool the chaos around her by ushering in a gentle, cooling breath. Though Ares is in charge of war, she would often step in to calm the wreckage his battles left behind by creating viable strategies for the soldiers to use to end the war. These divine tactics make her an incredible inspirational piece as well as a fierce contender in Greek mythology.

(This selection appears with permission from the author Kelli M. Webert, and was included as a Foreword in the work: *Athena, Queen of the Air* by John Ruskin, 2013 Annotated Version by TiLu Press.)

# *BAST, THE EGYPTIAN GODDESS (BASTET)*

Bastet is an influential goddess in Egyptian mythology, representing sensual pleasure. Bastet also acts as the guardian saint of firefighters, protector of the household and a bringer of wealth. Bastet may also be known as Bast, Bastethet or Bastetet and is widely represented as the cat goddess. Due to her role in protecting Ra, her father, from his enemies, she has also taken on the role of the All-Seeing Eye. This is occasionally represented as the Goddess of the Rising Sun or Lady of the East.

Bastet is one of the most ancient goddesses, she is depicted in many versions of Egyptian art. She is frequently depicted as a beautiful, slender woman with the head of a cat. The grounds of her temple hold a large cat cemetery where her companions could be mummified or entombed to join her in the spirit world. Cats are frequently honored at her temple, many taking up permanent residence. These cats were known to run into local homes when they caught fire, leading the residents to safety, which led to Bastet's association with fire-fighting and protection of the home. Some say that cats that lost their lives in this undertaking could be brought back to life by Bastet's power, which may be the source of the belief that cats have multiple lives.

During the day, Ra would fly through the sky, using his boat to pull the sun through the sky. When darkness falls Bastet transforms into a cat, taking advantage of the creature's superior night vision to watch for Apep, a serpent that acts as Ra's greatest enemy. Legend has it that Bastet was able to kill the serpent when the priests of Ra failed to hex him with the sacred wax models. Due to this dual nature of her story, Bastet is one of few sun goddesses that is also known as a moon goddess. Her sacred all-seeing eye reflects the light of the moon, protecting her followers from enemies in the darkness.

# *CIRCE*

Circe is a common figure in Greek mythology, though she has certainly taken on a variety of roles in different writings. In some cases she is depicted as an enchantress, sorceress, witch or nymph. Her role as a goddess is relatively minor compared to other figures more prominently depicted in the major mythological writings. Circe is known for having a wide knowledge of herbs and drugs. She would frequently use her wand and a variety of magical potions to transform those that offended her into animals.

This goddess is the daughter of the god of the sun Helios and an Oceanid Perse. Her siblings include Perses, Pasiphaie, wife of king Minos and mother to the Minotaur and Aeetes, the keeper of the Golden Fleece. Some writings depict her as the daughter of Hecate.

Stories surrounding the goddess frequently revolve around her murdering the prince of Colchis, her husband. When this happened, her subjects expelled Circe and her father onto the small island of Aeaea. In some later writings she is shown as destroying this island and running away to Italy, commonly to the area of Cape Circeo. Later literature depicts her as giving birth to Telegonus, Ardeas and Latinus, though legends vary regarding who the father of these children are.

Most know Circe for her role in Homer's Odyssey. When Odysseus and his crew found her mansion in a dense wood they noted that it was surrounded by wolves and lions that were strangely docile. Instead, they fawned on the newcomers while Circe worked at her loom. She invited the crew to partake of a meal that included cheeses and honey laced with wine. However, these foods also contained one of her potions which then transformed them into swine. Eurylochus suspected this treachery and ran away to warn Odysseus who was back at the ship so he could protect himself with an herb so he could confront her. After remaining on her island for a year, Circe offered Odysseus directions to the Underworld so he could continue his journey.

# *HERA, THE GREEK GODDESS OF MARRIAGE AND CHILDBIRTH*

Hera acts as the reigning queen of the gods in Greek mythology due to her role as Zeus's wife. (Her counterpart is the Roman Goddess Juno). Hera also acts as the goddess of marriage and childbirth. Because Zeus is also the god of philanderers, their natures would frequently clash. This has led to Hera being depicted as a quarrelsome and jealous goddess that can be a force to be reckoned with. In spite of her place as Zeus's bride, the worship of Hera is actually much older than that of her husband, stemming back to the days when the Greeks believed that any single entity associated with divinity must take the form of a woman. Her role is believed to have changed when the male's role in procreation became more understood, leading to Hera's worship as a mother figure rather than an all-encompassing deity.

Much of Hera's jealousy was directed toward women that Zeus seduced or had affairs with, though one of the most common legends associated with Hera is her jealousy toward the hero Hercules. This jealousy stemmed from the fact that Zeus fathered Hercules with the mortal Alcmene, a mortal. Hera went as far as to send snakes to kill Hercules when he was a baby. She also stirred the Amazons against him while he was on a quest.

Another famous legend associated with Hera has to do with the judgment of Paris. At the wedding between Peleus and Thetis (the later parents of Achilles) many gods and goddesses were invited to the ceremony. Eris, the goddess of discord, threw a golden apple among some of the goddesses, and only the fairest was to own the apple. Since Hera, Athena, and Aphrodite claimed to be the most beautiful goddess, a decision had to be made as to which goddess should own the apple. The goddesses brought the question before Zeus, but. Zeus was wise enough to leave the choice of who was the most beautiful goddess up to Paris, a Trojan prince. So the three Goddesses, Hera, Athena, and Aphrodite came before Paris, but he could not decide. Finally, each of them offered Paris a gift to try to persuade him. It is said that Athena offered him great fame and glory in battle, Hera offered him control over all of Asia and Europe, and Aphrodite offered him the most beautiful mortal woman in the world. Because of this he chose Aphrodite, which absolutely enraged the other two goddesses, especially Hera. Of course the most beautiful woman in the world at that time was Helen of Troy who was already married to the King of Sparta. So after the abduction of Helen by Paris, there was a great war (partially stored up by the jealous goddesses); and this was called the Trojan War.

There is some debate surrounding Hera's familial roles. Some origin stories depict Hera's parents as the Titans Rhea and Cronus, making her Zeus's sister. Given these close family ties, there is some debate on whether or not Zeus and Hera produced children together. Hera is known as the lone parent of Hephaestus. Ares and Hebe are often depicted as the children of Zeus and Hera, but in some traditions Ares is seen to have been conceived from a flower in the field of Olenus and Hebe fathered by a lettuce. These tales may have been invented to avoid adding scandal to Hera's myth.

In any regard, the Greek goddess Hera is a major part of Goddess mythologies and motifs. She is not only a fierce mother image, but also that of the fierce, powerful wife, and symbolizes both a wifely devotion towards her husband, and respect for the protection of marriage.

# *ISIS, THE EGYPTIAN MOTHER GODDESS OF PROTECTION*

Isis is the Egyptian patron saint of magic and nature. Isis appears as protector of children and a protector of the dead. She is commonly depicted as being a friend to artists, sinners, slaves and the downtrodden, though she would also listen to the prayers of rulers, aristocrats, the wealthy and maidens.

Isis is the mother of Horus, the god of protection and war. Her name literally translates to "throne" and she wears a throne on her head to depict this, though it is believed that she was seen as a wife or assistant to deceased pharaohs in the Old Kingdom. She acts as a symbol of the power of the pharaoh, and the current pharaoh would frequently be depicted as her child, sitting on her throne. The myth of Isis became exceptionally popular in the Greco-Roman period, though the image of Isis mothering the leader of the Egyptian world was translated to an image of Mary suckling her son Jesus as the Christians moved to suppress *pagan* religions.

Temples to Isis were built throughout Rome, Iraq and Greece, though it was understood that Isis remained with her husband Osiris in Egypt. These temples would become home to healers believed to have special powers to control the weather or interpret dreams which was accessed by braiding the hair in a special way. The cult of Isis widely believed that knots held special power which could be accessed by adorning your body with them. Very little about the rituals of the Isis cult is known because they were disbanded during the Greco-Roman area.

It was frequently believed that her tears would cause the Nile River to flood. Isis would weep for the death of Osiris as he died and would become reborn each year, contributing to the flooding cycle that occurred each spring. Her cult remained quite local to this area, even after Egyptian mythology proceeded to spread to further reaches of the kingdom. Egypt is seen as her home, though she would see leaders on to the afterlife in some depictions. Isis is considered the mother of the four sons of Horus, the deities in charge of protecting the canopic jars which held a pharaoh's internal organs after death.

Isis was especially associated with Imesty, the protector of the liver jar.

In the New Kingdom, the role of Isis evolved as the cult of Ra rose in prominence. Ra was paired with Horus, and since Isis was paired with Horus, she rose in prominence throughout the ancient world. During this time, the myth of Isis and Osiris became one of the most important myths in Egyptian culture. Set murdered his brother Osiris in order to usurp the throne. Osiris's wife Isis, brokenhearted, restored her husband's body so she could conceive a son with him posthumously. This son was Horus, who would frequently battle Set for the throne, a battle which eventually became victorious. As Horus became the protector and representation of the pharaoh, Isis became the protector of the pharaoh who would see him to victory in his endeavors.

# *KALI, HINDU FIERCE MOTHER GODDESS*

Kali, also known as the Dark Mother, is a ferocious form of the mother goddess which can be quite fearful as well. Those who are devoted to this goddess can form a very deep and intimate bond despite the fearful and intense appearance of this goddess. Kali takes her followers in, assuming the mother role and treating them as her children.

She is one of the first of ten Mahavidyas in the Hindu tradition. Others include Shodashi, Bhuvaneshwari, Tara, Chinnamasta, Bhairavi, Matangi, Dhumavati, Bugala Muki and Kamala. Due to this association, Kali is also known as Adya in her first-born form. These goddesses represent the ten essential energies that bring about the ten essential insights sought through the main paths of Tantra Yoga. Kali, the first of these goddesses teaches that life seems temporary, but in reality both time and life are endless. Death is merely an illusion that the

Kali mantra can be used to overcome. Those that choose to follow this mantra must be willing to give up their attachment to the body. This helps her followers remove the insecurity associated with the first Chakra, or fears located in the primitive brain and brain stem.

Kali is the consort of Lord Shiva, and is often depicted standing on Shiva's form. Placing her foot on Shiva subdues her anger. Her name translates to *the black one*, referring to the fact that she is an entity that is beyond time. Kali is depicted with black coloring as a contrast to Shiva, symbolizing the time that was created with her manifested in her creation.

The Dark Mother is most well-known for sending the Mother Gauri Shakti to free the other gods from the demonic clutches of Nishumbh and Shumbh when these forces conquered the celestial plane, astral plane and earth, establishing her place as one of the foremost goddesses in Hindu culture.

# *KWAN YIN, THE GODDESS OF COMPASSION*

With her origins still being debated over, we can at least attest that Kwan means to inquire deeply and that Yin means to cry. This goddess is shown in many forms, but they all show her unique compassion and mercy. Many times you can see Kwan Yin as a slender woman in flowing white robes carrying a white lotus in her left hand which is a representation of purity and the ideal of womanhood. She might also be seen wearing ornaments to show her stature, or without them to show how modest she is.

Kwan Yin is also known as a "bringer of children". Because of this, many images of her can be seen in homes and temples. In these instances, a large white veil will be covering her whole body and she could be seated on a lotus, rather than carrying one. Instead, a child will be in her arms, or the child will be seated near her. Sometimes you can see her with several children at once, which she is then known to be the "white-robed honored one".

Many times you will see Kwan Yin with several hands, heads and eyes, plus a thousand arms. In the palms of each of her hands there will sometimes be an eye. This symbolizes her as the omnipresent "Divine Mother" being able to see in all directions at once and therefore all the problems of humanity. In this image she reaches out to everyone with her extreme compassion and mercy to help console all.

# *LAKSHMI, HINDU GODDESS AND HER PUJA*

Lakshmi puja is a ritual celebrated during Diwali, or the festival of lights. The ritual is dedicated to showing propitiation and devotion to Lakshmi, the goddess of fortune, wealth, prosperity and the embodiment of beauty. Lakshmi is known to bring good luck to her believers and devotees, rescuing them from money troubles and other miseries. She is frequently worshipped and honored as a goddess of wealth in commercial establishments or homes. Lakshmi is also honored as the consort of Vishnu, which has endowed her with six divine qualities.

Because Lakshmi is seen as one who takes light in, she is an important figure in the Diwali festival. It is said that those looking to honor the goddess would light lanterns outside their home in hopes that they would draw the Lakshmi in to bless them. The third day of Diwali is the most important day of Lakshmi puja because the sun will enter its second course, allowing Libra to assist with the balancing the books and closing records, bringing Lakshmi additional power to bless her followers. The first days of this festival are also celebrated with drums and bells to represent the "pouring in" of the heart, expressing the thanks for the many blessings and prosperity Lakshmi has brought.

A number of elements are considered essential to the rite of celebrating Lakshmi puja. In the temples, a cloth is placed across a raised platform and an alter is made with grains, pitchers made from terracotta, gold, silver or copper, a dish of rice grains, a lotus flower drawn in turmeric and an idol of Lakshmi surrounded by coins. The idol is bathed in water and panchamrit, followed by a second bath in water infused with gold or pearls. She is then wiped clean and the water is sprinkled on the turmeric lotus to invoke the goddess. Businesses may include books related to their profession around the altar as well as these traditional elements.

Households will place a lantern or make offerings of kumkum, flowers or haldi to the goddess. Offerings of cotton beads, flowers such as marigolds, apple wood, sandal paste, perfume and sandal paste are also frequently offered. After these initial offerings are given, incense is lit to purify the altar. Then a second offering of fruits, coconut, sweets, tambul, puffed rice, coriander, cumin and batasha are given. These elements are not to be mixed with the honey or jewelry on the altar out of respect to Lord Kuber.

Prayers to Lakshmi are frequently recited during the Lakshmi puja celebration. Groups will perform aarti (Hindu religious worship) for the goddess, though these celebrations are often quieter than traditional celebrations as Lakshmi is not fond of loud noises. Instead, small bells are used to accompany the prayers and aarti. Unlike aarti that are performed for other gods, groups should not clasp hands when performing this ritual, nor should firecrackers be set off during or after the puja. Homes should strive to keep a sublime, peaceful and comforting atmosphere out of respect to the goddess and her celebration during Diwali.

# *MA DURGA, HINDU GODDESS AS MAHADEVI*

Ma Durga, or the Durga mother, is the fierce form of the goddess Devi in the Hindu tradition. She is often associated with Mahadevi, the supreme goddess for her defeat of Mahishasura Mardini the buffalo demon. Ma Durga is frequently portrayed with multiple arms, which can be as many as eighteen in some interpretations. She is also frequently portrayed riding a tiger or lion or using weapons to slay demons as a show of her power. Many portraits relate the story of her victory over Mardini, showing her slaying him or holding off his forces as they attack.

The legend of Ma Durga first appears on the narrative of Devi Mahatmya within the text of the Markandeya Purana. According to legend, Ma Durga was created in the image of a warrior goddess to help fight the asura Mashishasura. The warrior gods were ineffective against this demon because Brahma had blessed Mashishasura with the power to be un-defeatable at the hands of man or god. To counter-act this magic, Shiva requested that his wife Parvati take on a role where she could take on this demon. While she called upon the priests at Vaikuntha, Shiva tried to hold off Mashishasura and his forces by combining the three lead gods and emitting a beam of light.

Though the gods were defeated, this light reached Parvati at Vaikuntha, alerting the gods here. To save the three worlds, they combined forces to create a new pool of light. From this light rose Ma Durga, the female aspect of Brahman, a lila that emerged from their combined energy and com-passion.

As she moved forward to battle Mashishasur, he made the mistake of underestimating her power, thinking that a woman could not possibly defeat him after he had defeated a trinity of gods. To show his strength, he changed forms many times as he rampaged toward Ma Durga, appearing as a buffalo demon, an elephant, a lion and a man. Ma Durga is said to have gracefully defeated each of these forms. In his last charge, Mashishasur returned to his buffalo form, but became trapped between this and the form of a man. Laughing at his predicament, Ma Durga cut him down with her sword, ending the battle and cementing her compassion in the hearts of her followers.

According to some versions of the legend, Ma Durga raised an army to march against Mahishasur as he terrorized heaven and earth. This battle raged on for ten days before she took it upon herself to slay this demon king. As a reward for their good service, Ma Durga rewarded her troops with the knowledge for jewelry-making. Because of this gift, Ma Durga is frequently depicted in art pieces. She is often represented covered in stones and jewels, even in scenes which act out the tale of her decapitating the buffalo demon. This act of bravery and compassion is also worshiped widely in many parts of the Himalayan region and throughout India, especially during the ten day period when the battle was said to have commenced.

# *MA DURGA, MY ENCOUNTER WITH THE BENEVOLENT MOTHER*

Although there are different manifestations of the Hindu goddess Ma Durga, such as Lakshmi, Parvati, and Durga herself, it is my encounter with Ma Durga as a mother figure that has made a lasting impression upon me.

For as she gathers those that need help in her arms of compassion, and leads them gently from times of trouble, her caring is so apparent. For it is as a gentle mother and caring one that She leads me to safety and protection that resonates so deeply within me again and again. For as we humans well know, we needn't go looking for troubles, sometimes they will find us! Never do we need the touch and care of a friend more, a companion, a brother or sister in dialogue--the caring of family and loved ones--as it is then that the gentle leading of the archetypal Mother Goddess is ever needed!

And thank goodness, when called upon She arises, and gathers us in Her arms. And yet, She does not wait to be called upon--for like any good Mother she responds to our distress.

Her eyes are certainly seeking, searching, and settling upon those in times of trouble, they are gentle, reassuring, and if need be, drawing us to attention.

Her smile is as the dripping honey on the lotus. She warms the hearts of all India, and the world.

This tiger riding Goddess is the ultimate mother!

Several years ago, I had a deeply meaningful and especially vivid dream about Ma Durga. I knew right away in my dream who she was and what the dream was about. I could tell the woman in the dream was Ma Durga because of her attire, her Goddess face, and those eyes that only Ma Durga has!

Anyway, in this dream that I readily recalled upon sudden awakening at its conclusion, the events went like this. I entered a supermarket, and I felt like I was lost from someone, or had gone ahead of someone. But I also felt ashamed, like I was 'in trouble', or had done something that I felt 'stupid' about. I felt like a kid who had done something wrong, but didn't want his parents to know. I was a grown man in the dream however.

So I went down the shopping aisles filled with all

sorts of foods and plenty of them. I came upon the glass enclosed cold storage units, the units where they keep frozen packaged products like pizzas, ice cream, frozen dinners, etc. Well, I climbed up on top of one of these units, and laid down flat on my back. I lay down as flat as I could, so as not to be readily or easily seen by anyone who might enter the store or was walking nearby. From where I was, I could turn my head and see the main entry of the store how-ever.

So for some reason, I turned my head towards the entry doors. It was if I was waiting for someone, anticipating someone coming, but I didn't know for sure who it would be.

Suddenly, I saw Ma Durga come through the doors. She was walking towards my location! I tried to melt into the metal of the casing so as not to be seen. But there was to be no hiding, as she lovingly approached. She was a fully radiant being, and was smiling as she approached, her eyes was taking in everything around her. As she came closer, she grew and magically became taller. As she got to where I was, she was now taller than the enclosures, and easily saw me.

She looked at me with so much love and accept-ance, my heart melted. It was if her eyes could see everything about me, accepted me, forgave all my troubles, or made them all vanish in the manifest-ation of Her power. In that one look, was all this and much more instantaneously. Love, acceptance, for-giveness, and reassurance!

She calmly put her hands on her hips, looked into my eyes with her Ma Durga Eyes, and She said: "Well, are you coming? Get down from there and follow me!"

I hopped down and immediately left with her out of the store with all of its materialism and wealth, and happily followed Her. The joy and relief was enormous! I then awoke with a start.

This dream deeply resonated with me, although I knew I was a mature man in the dream, her loving approach to me elicited both a son like sense, and also a childlike sense. I knew I had done something, and felt like I might be in trouble. So I was trying hard to hide from 'Mom'.

Still, when Ma Durga 'found' me, I was overcome by several feelings at once, love, acceptance, and reassurance. I expected wrath, but got deep love. I also knew I was totally safe with her, protected, and that all my troubles were solved and no longer as important as I had thought they were. So I was eager and readily able to hop down and follow her out of the store. Happily returning to everyday life and then, transcending the world, protected by the Goddess, I suddenly awoke with this realization deeply embedded in my consciousness.

It was a wonderful experience, and although some people think dreaming is just the firing of neurons, that dream was one of the most meaning-ful dreams I've ever had.

# *PARVATI, HINDU GODDESS OF LOVE AND DEVOTION*

Also known as the daughter of the mountain, the goddess Parvati's story might indeed be one of the most interesting of goddesses. She was born out of need as the gods need the assistance of the God Shiva. Shiva, however, had holed himself up in a mountain cave of the Himalayas, doing nothing but meditating and performing tapas to mourn the loss of his first love. His heat and energy grew and grew, and he became full of knowledge.

So the goddess Shakti went into his cave, some stories say appearing as a serpent and coiled herself around Shiva to draw out his energy and power so he would father a child, as the gods knew that only a child born of Shiva would be powerful enough to help them. Shakti than birthed herself into the goddess Parvati and her main goal was to win Shiva's affections.

Even as a child she was deeply in love with him and went to his cave every day to sweep and decorate it with flowers. Shiva, however, never once noticed her, and could not be brought out of his mediations. So she invoked the help of Priti and Rati, who changed the cave into a thing of beauty, and then brought the lord of desire, Kama, to Shiva, but Shiva destroyed him by shooting flames from his third eye.

Having lost the lord of desire, the gods were hopeless of what to do with Shiva. Parvati then took off to go to the woods with nothing, not even clothing, to meditate and learn tapas, until her strength grew to that of Shiva's and he took notice of her finally and took her as his wife, which also restored Kama back to life.

# *PERSEPHONE, GREEK GODDESS OF THE UNDERWORLD*

Persephone is known as the Greek goddess of the underworld and the wife of Hades. Before this she was the goddess of the spring. She is the daughter of Zeus and Demeter the goddess of the harvest. As the legend goes, Persephone was so beautiful that all men desired her for their wife. Hades became so enthralled by the goddess that he determined he must have her for his own. One day Persephone was out picking flowers and the gates of the underworld opened around her and abducted the goddess. Helios the all-seeing sun and Zeus stood witness.

After Persephone was kidnapped, Demeter was frantic. She wandered the earth searching for her lost daughter. Feeling sorry for her, Helios told her where her daughter had gone. Demeter was furious upon learning that Hades had stolen her daughter away and hid herself out of loneliness and despair. During this time the world lost its ability to grow crops. Concerned that this would put the world in peril, Zeus sent Hermes into Hades, ordering him to set Persephone free. Hades agreed, but cunningly offered Persephone a pomegranate before she left. Some legends claim he simply offered her pomegranate seeds before her departure.

After returning home, Persephone ate the seeds of the pomegranate, binding herself to the underworld permanently. Not wanting to give up her daughter forever, Demeter struck a deal with Hades. Persephone would spend part of the year on earth with her mother and the remaining portion of each year in the underworld as the bride of Hades. This represents the cycle of the seasons each year. When Persephone leaves for Hades to fulfill her portion of the obligation, Demeter is too heartbroken to allow anything to grow and winter comes. As Persephone makes her reappearance, spring appears and everything blooms anew.

# *SARASWATI, THE ARTISTIC HINDU GODDESS*

For every Indian artist, the goddess Saraswati is a major influence. To them, all art–old and new – starts with Saraswati. She is the Hindu goddess of music, knowledge and creative arts and is also known as Vak Devi, or the goddess of speech.

Originally from the creation of the goddess that Brahma fashioned after himself of whom half was woman and half was man. The woman part of this goddess was called Gayatri, but later she became known by several other names, one of them being Saraswati.

She appears always in all white and usually is seen riding atop a swan, but sometimes can be seen on a peacock instead. She plays music on a veena, and holds in her hands a mala, or prayer beads, and a palm leaf scroll to show knowledge.

Indian students take the power of Saraswati very seriously, and a daily mantra can be recited to supposedly improve their concentration, memory and power in their studies. They regularly worship Saraswati in hopes to do well on their tests, as well. There is a temple, Vilma Vashi, which is solely dedicated to Saraswati.

In yoga, Saraswati is represented as the neutral channel in a trio that also includes the lunar energy channel which symbolizes the river Ganga and the solar energy channel which represents the river and the Yamuna goddess. Then the upward flow of the Kundalini goes straight through the central channel, Saraswati, to pierce the chakras and bring liberation. This convergence is called Triveni Sangam and takes place near Allahabad.

In summary, general aspects of the Goddess Saraswati includes her status as the wife (consort) of Lord Brahma and the fact that it is she that possesses the powers of speech, wisdom and learning. She has four hands representing four aspects of human personality in learning; mind, intellect, alertness and ego.

She has sacred scriptures in one hand and a lotus (a symbol of true knowledge) in the second. With her other two hands she plays the music of love and life on the violin (veena). There are other goddesses similar in appearance and characteristics to Saraswati. Some researchers say that the Asian goddess Benzaiten is also related to this goddess.

# *A FEW GODDESS POEMS BY TIM KAVI*

Goddesses play a pivotal role in much of my poetry, which appears regularly on the same blog as my *More About Goddesses* essay columns. I've also had published two poetry collections, *Emerging Goddess* (2011) and *Ascending Goddess* (2012) that feature Goddess themed poetry. At least two more Goddess collections are planned. Here's a sampling of some of my Goddess poems.

# MA DURGA'S EYES

Ma Durga's Eyes
have over all time
cried thousands of cries
and uttered thousands of sighs

but none are more beautiful than my love's

her eyes have lit a thousand ships
home to harbor
have touched my lips
across many trips

her eyes are so wise.

Ma Durga's Eyes
I need you so
to them I always go
to see the world
and each other.

there are no other eyes I know
I will return again and again
to her heart to go.

My love's eyes
are Ma Durga's Eyes

her heart so true
that the eyes are all telling
of her many stories
from the countryside are yelling
out of the rocks and hills
the majestic spills
of water cascading down the falls
while the rest of the world waits in their alls
we hear the love in her calls.

Ma Durga's Eyes of my love
of yesteryear and then
I knew them before
somehow
on another shore
but when I saw them again
her Ma Durga's Eyes were different than then
her eyes are so wise.

Ma Durga's Eyes
I need you so
to them I always go
to see the world
and each other.

my lovely Sweet love
Ma Durga's Eyes
light where we have ever been
and they touch my heart so
where the Himalayan winds blow
and the currents of Ganges do flow

she is ever present in the wind

against the wind
she stands still

her eyes are so wise.

Ma Durga's Eyes
I need you so
to them I always go
to see the world
and each other.

Ma Durga's Eyes through history
tell many stories
they begin and end with my lovely love.

# ATHENA'S LAUREL CALLS MY JOURNEYED SOUL

oh I didn't know you were close to me
I thought it was just the stardust
or the whispering sea
I can see you still talk to me

across the history
glimpsing you
I thought I saw
a memory

there is only
the laurel leaves
scattered by the wind
where Owl watches over me

that is where the gentle
sounds of our love misgiven
led to bad steps

and misplaced heaven
the day the winged bird
took you away from me

I began the mountainous climb
a journey to the sacred heart
longing left me famished
my song carried no more rhyme

spirits were broken
the people were wandering
in the valley below
the shepherds were themselves lost
the leaders blinded by the dark
and the prisoners remained chained
against the rock

only the annointed ones
dare come up here
olive oil burns not only the lamp
but annoints my forehead

I cry out like a madman
there is no one to hear me
it echoes against the rocks
where lumber is free
from too many shipwrecks
skeletal hands clutching for
your Grecian shore

I try to find you
but in the darkness
you are not found anymore

what greatness is this?
your temples once majestic
lined a path upwards
up high to a cloudy
celestial throne
where once you blew me a kiss!

How did I know that kiss
was a good bye kiss
to me and the world?

now there is only ruin
return to Your Greatness
perhaps men will yet invoke
your name
rebuilding temples won't be the same

but there is still power
in the virtues
of your name

oh a calling
a certain shrill
breaks the night
and my stubborn will

I will climb up higher
I will look for you
and I will kiss you again
and again

can you imagine
how much I missed you?

your glory as a woman
is everywhere
yet the priests stop and stare
but in your Goddess face
is only the visitations
of everlasting grace

your look is on them too
that woman just killed
the male shame
of violence
makes me want to jump
off this hill

hear the words
priests too
the hour is late
there is much to do
respect Athena
and all her sisters
or tales of woe
will never be few

I will burn my skin
and twist my robe
pluck hairs from my head
pray pray pray
until the truth be said

stop my sisters'
blood running red!
Athena has now said!

so here I sit all night
your tears watered
pools at my feet
I can only bow my head and worship
Goddess come back
we are so sorry that some have hurt you

wear your laurel wreath again
entreaty forgive our sin
you think you bad ones can easily make right
but your weapons
and hate
and violence
must go away...

for Athena comes
in sacred flight.

# LOVE AMONG
# THE RUINS

Oh Goddess

your ancient
images
lie among the ruins
many miles
from here

Hai goddess

some thought you were
shattered

your lingering
presentness
makes
your conspicuous
absence increased
by the eternal
tears

Hai goddess

others thought in love
you were tattered

your resonant songs
were still sung
in children's rhymes
and beautiful
portraits
that their mothers hung

Hai goddess

they and I sought you
like You mattered

until
one breathes
and it is
already a decade
or two
amongst memory
who cares how many years

For You live
and live
and live

and will never die

still there
in the ruins
clothed priests
of the newer traditions

thought there
is only gatherings
between your wooings

but
Hai goddess

soon you sleep no more
arise from
the ashes of slumber
I rebuild your statues

but they look
like a real woman

in the moonlight

as we love
among the ruins.

# ABOUT THE AUTHOR

## Tim Kavi

Tim Kavi is an American born poet and mystic who writes about the Goddess, love, and personal freedom. His work celebrates the capacities of human beings to love, and to make changes in their lives that are positive and transformational. He believes that genuine dialogue, dialectical thinking, and a quest for wholeness are important aspects of human development. As a result of multiple university degrees and experiences, Kavi has worked as a counselor, businessman, and consultant. In poetry, he is most well known for his Goddess poetry collections where he celebrates the Sacred Feminine and emerging goddesses everywhere with love poems. He has been published with three prior collections: Emerging Goddess (2011),Lost Love Poems (2012) and Ascending Goddess (2012). Forthcoming collections include: Poems of Protest, City of Night/City of Light, and Revealed Goddess.

Official Home Page of Tim Kavi: http://www.tim-kavipoet.com

You can follow him and his current work through his writing blog at: http://www.timkavi.blog-spot.com

Twitter: http://www.twitter.com/TimKavi

Facebook: http://www.facebook.com/TimKavi

www.ingramcontent.com/pod-product-compliance
Lightning Source LLC
Chambersburg PA
CBHW061518250726
48657CB00005B/1931